The Lord is My Shepherd

Illustrated by Regolo Ricci

TUNDRA BOOKS

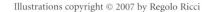

Illustrations copyright © 2007 by Regolo Ricci

Published in Canada by Tundra Books,
75 Sherbourne Street, Toronto, Ontario M5A 2P9

Published in the United States by Tundra Books of Northern New York,
P.O. Box 1030, Plattsburgh, New York 12901

Library of Congress Control Number: 2006908556

Library and Archives Canada Cataloguing in Publication

Bible.   O.T.   Psalms XXIII.   English.   Authorized.   2006
        The Lord is my shepherd / Regolo Ricci.

ISBN 978-0-88776-776-0

        I. Ricci, Regolo   II. Title.

BS1450 23rd.B43 2007   223'.2052034   C2006-905500-9

We acknowledge the financial support of the Government of Canada through
the Book Publishing Industry Development Program (BPIDP) and that of the
Government of Ontario through the Ontario Media Development Corporation's
Ontario Book Initiative. We further acknowledge the support of the Canada Council
for the Arts and the Ontario Arts Council for our publishing program.

ONTARIO ARTS COUNCIL
CONSEIL DES ARTS DE L'ONTARIO

The text of Psalm 23 for this edition is based on the King James Version of the Bible.
The paintings for this book were rendered in watercolor on illustration board.

Design: Terri Nimmo and Regolo Ricci

Printed and bound in China

1 2 3 4 5 6   12 11 10 09 08 07

for Mindy Ravinsky

he Lord is my shepherd,
I shall not want.

He maketh me to lie down in green pastures;

He leadeth me beside the still waters.
He restoreth my soul.

e leadeth me in the paths of righteousness for his name's sake.

ea, though I walk through
the valley of the shadow
of death, I will fear no evil;

or thou art with me,
thy rod and thy staff,
they comfort me.

hou preparest a table
before me in the presence
of mine enemies.

hou annointest my head with oil; my cup runneth over.

urely goodness and mercy
shall follow me all the days
of my life,

nd I will dwell in the house of the Lord forever.